To Virginia T. —

my town

poems by steven rydman

8/5/03

Grovers
Corners
Press

PLEASANT RIDGE, MI
A proud part of the Emerging Ink Collective

contents

I

II

III

for all the saints and poets in my life

Emily:	Do any human beings ever realize life while they live it - every, every minute?
Stage Manager:	No - Saints and poets maybe - they do some.

-Thornton Wilder: *Our Town*

I

Out of My Mother

She always reaches in as if bones
are easier to touch than skin.
We're watching the Grammy's
together on the velour couch
the gas heat barely melting
the awkward chill between us.

"Are you gay?" she asks, the question
left hanging in the air like smoke
from a chimney, a trail to fire.

"Yes," I say, holding my chin up,
the way I did in her womb.
Made me stay inside her three more weeks.
Maybe she wishes I hadn't come out.

Silence, like before a storm or a crash,
presses on my cheeks as they flush.
Her plump hands, smoothed by years of praying,
touch them gently, while her voice
full of its stern softness
fills with the relief of finally pushing
a growing part of yourself out into the world.

"I'm glad I named you Steven,"
she says, "For strength, courage."

Stained-Glass Jesus

The Son doesn't want to cause sadness
in Jesus' eyes: perfect black spots of iron
dripped on a sullen face, its rainbow of glass shapes
lined with crude metal, muted as it hangs
on the beige suburban wall. If Jesus cries,
both eyes will tumble down his sunken cheeks
and something in Father's drunken stagger
tells the boy he is the cause of everything.
So he tiptoes a lot, tries to melt into gold carpet
like an ice cube in Father's whiskey glass.
Mother glances daily at Jesus.
She zips her boots, draws small gloves
over smooth hands. It's a choreographed genuflect to Him,
her head swaddled in a white scarf.
Sometimes, she cradles the Son's face in her gloved hands
calls him her "little old man." A kiss on the forehead
anoints him with an ashy pink mark.
She floats through the house
places a pine cone wreath to frame Jesus' face
sprinkles it with white lights,
fake red berries that light up and blush
like Jesus' pulsing heart, balanced above His hands held in prayer.
Christmas Eve night, the Son crawls
into cold sheets between Mother and Father.
This space, that he knows is never crossed,
is a crib for him, surrounded in the tawny hay
of whiskey breath and Mother's soft white belly.
In the morning, the Son beams
darting between pointed shadows
of Father's drunken fingers. Excitement twinkles
like the rainbow of lights on the tree.
In this pale glow, Jesus' grim face sparkles with sinister color
trapped in frigid metal and the cones' brown spikes.
The eyes follow the Son, their metal an icy weight
on the top of his head, the nape of his neck.
They follow, no matter how fast
he runs in circles around the family room
bows and ribbons dangling from his pajamas.

Suppose at Twelve, I Am Not a Boy

But instead, I am a spring leaf
leaning easily on another leaf
drops of sap sticking between us
my chartreuse veins preening
against moist green skin.

Or I am a stamen in a calla lily,
a proud golden rod
gently rubbing tawny dust
on smooth alabaster petals.

Yes, my father's callused palm
is just the brown scratch of bark
protecting with its harsh stroke.

And my mother is a dense thicket
of bushes and pachysandra
cradling our footsteps
and covering the dirt.

Or suppose I am just a boy
with a family of dry stick figures
pressed in black ink
next to a crayon colored house,
crumpled and thrown away
with a child's impatience.

Lover Come Back

Allen haunts me
in the closets of my dreams.
With a wink and a smile
he whispers *Send me no flowers*
and closes the unending doors
between us.

In his sons' beds on sleepovers,
I listened between paper walls to his pillow talk,
stolen from the TV screen,
whispering words from "McMillan and Wife"
to the mother of his seven kids.
He was a giant in his living room,
July sun beaming, its white light
erasing teeth marks from baby bottles
balanced against his chest
in a pink triangle from his bare arms
to the dimple in his chin.
Always, a Sunday smile plastered
over his tired face, glistening
like a plastic-wrapped TV dinner.
Alone, my fingers flirted
through a rainbow of Izod shirts
lining his closet for morning golf.

Once, on a summer trip to Petosky,
he kept me company in the cabin's humid kitchen.
The boys outside playing some sport.
A leather ball bouncing between their shouts
like words to a karaoke song I couldn't follow.
Allen says *You're a good kid*,
holding his beer can with one pinky in the air,
like a Rock Hudson movie moment
when he feigns gay to get closer to Doris Day.
His other hand shaking above my naked shoulder.

The Good Sisters

We make our way into the world
cradled by our parents' smoke rings
swimming in poisonous blood.
A plastic flask of vodka tucked in a pocket

cradled by our own smoke rings,
we choke on our first inhale.
A plastic flask of vodka tucked in a pocket,
two sisters lost in the swirl of alcohol,

we choke on our first swallow.
Partying late into nights without curfews,
two sisters lost in the swirl of alcohol
like calves stumbling on drunken legs.

We party late into nights without curfews,
sinking down cheap backseats of sweaty nylon
like calves stumbling on drunken legs.
We collect strangers' semen like precious diamonds

sinking down cheap backseats of sweaty nylon.
Tattoos burn initials into broken arms.
We collect strangers' semen like precious diamonds
waiting for one who'll slip a ring on wetted finger.

Tattoos burn initials into broken arms
swimming in poisonous blood
waiting for one who'll slip a ring on wetted finger
we make our way into the world.

Grandma Emma, From Pictures

It seems your hair was always white.
Mom says you were mostly afraid, and I imagine
you woke one night, lying rigid in bed
your husband banging his whiskey breath
through the house. He drags your daughter from bed
dangles her upside down in your dark doorway,
swinging back and forth like a languid pendulum
flicking his sluggish slurs at both of you.

The next morning, you look in the mirror
the color drained from your black hair,
white face now splintered with dark veins,
wide eyes barely able to blink, afraid
of what ticks in that darkness.

If we had met, I think I could have brought
the color back. On a porch in Cheboygan,
I would have sat at the foot of your rocking chair
house so quiet with all his rage buried
deep in the brown ground. You knit and rock,
fall in and out of sleep. I push red cars
around your bare feet, giggle
and scrunch my nose at the yellow corns
under your toes, the pale purple spider webs
around your ankles.

I'd never know the cold
my mom speaks about you,
because on our porch
in its dim, dim quiet,
I'd hear your heart snap open
and fill that empty house
with the sun's white hot light.

Familiar Objects

Her house is a dead end today.
Sun can't wake up, taking all afternoon
to light a dim bulb behind a gauze of clouds.
A spring gray spreads rain over magnolia buds
their bruised centers trying to bloom.
The woman's hand gropes at tangled cords, can't plug in a hair dryer.
Frustrated, a leak of tears falls from her red eyes,
two relentless bath taps weeping
no matter how hard she twists them off
a hundred tugs to stop the dripping.
She wanders abandoned streets in her house,
hair wet like a heavy hat of black snow.
In the bedroom closet, her old wedding shoes
glow like satin moons. She slips them on
to click through the cotton silence stuffed in her ears.
The phone rings. She ticks down the stairs
naked across sticky linoleum
but can't pick up the receiver,
afraid her desperate hello will be greeted
by the moan of a dial tone.
A trickle of light through sheer curtains
flickers like candlelight along the ceiling.
Her heavy head falls back as she blows at each sparkle
as if snuffing a flame before lowering onto a lover's body.
And then, there it is, empty on the counter:
her glass, waiting for the rusty storm of whisky,
the clear, summer shower of vodka,
even the autumn drizzle of beer
could pour into her dry mouth,
flood her scorched throat
and before she knows it, she's filling the glass
and gulping and gulping and gulping
like a sun scorched traveler who finds an oasis in the desert.

In her last swallow, the house fills to its brim
with the ghosts of old lovers
raising threadbare arms to toast her drunken redemption.
Six glasses later, they all leave her
again and again, but she doesn't care, her body fallen
like the browned magnolia petals sprinkled on the lawn.

At the Airport

The woman waits, her dog
sleeping in its boxed cage
at her feet. His shocked fur
lit like a bulb of tan light
reaches for a freedom
that waits outside the bars.
The sun's light slants on her face
as it sets in the west. She will fly,
north, to a dark home,
a sleeping husband. She won't wake him
as she sits by a cracked bedroom window
the flamed tendrils of her red hair
reaching for her reflection
in the smudged glass.

La Fin du Monde

Like rows of coffins, fluorescent lights
line the ceiling, processionals of dead light.
One casket is mine, and I float up into it.
A polyester warmth sizzles around me
a hot shower on fresh sunburn
though my skin is cold,
a blizzard of cerulean snow and shadow.
A pale girl wipes coffee tables around me.
Her blue hair hangs like apocalyptic icicles
creating a blue corona of light to crown her.
She wakes me from my wordless coma.
I ask: *What is the most exciting thing you've seen today?*
Her face blank as the page I write on.
I'll give you two, she says, *coffee grounds and dust bunnies.*
The scratchy needle of boredom
skipping in her mouth.
Au revoir, c'est la fin du monde!
She circles away; her white rag erasing everything.
I drift up to the ceiling again
into my blazing coffin.
Au revoir, le monde! Au revoir!
Light caresses skin, a satin lining I lie in
my eyes buried in dusty white clouds
that glow and grow into mouth, melt on my tongue
like rocks of sugar. An artificial buzz rings
the choked whispers of mourners as they pass beneath me,
the heat of their perfumed air rising to my lit nostrils.

13th Street Nursery Rhyme

13th street Philly garbage swirls
around Tyrell. He reads street signs
his 7-year-old articulations
sound out McDougal and Watts
like most kids say home.

He learns that math is the means to figure
out the amount his Mama couldn't afford
for rent and heat and the habit because
she screams how the crack shell hides her
30-year-old young eyes.

Her sons crouch in abandon corners of
buildings with black hole windows
paying her bills and playing daddy singing
"Humpty Dumpty sat on a wall."

A wall cluttered with crushed Coors Lite cans and
condom wrappers, crack vials, bright white shards of
plaster from the broken home it surrounds.
"Humpty Dumpty had a great fall."

Tyrell sighs at the shards and sees
sunny buds rise from a crack in the wall,
wants to bring a little gold to his mother,
dandelions to delight her growing days.

Tyrell wants to pick up the pieces the world
left his mother in because he already knows
the king's horses and the king's men couldn't
even put Humpty back together again.

Small Talk

At another acquaintance's birthday party, surrounded by a
quaintness of red brick and manufactured smiles, I'm asked
again, So what do you do? I write poetry, my occupation lands
on plush white carpet like a red Chianti stain. Everyone
shocked, but trying not to ask how it happened. The conversa-
tion walks around it. A man who is all periods and commas (at
best, a dramatic ellipse) shifts into a diatribe about gas, gas
prices, his leather oxfords soaked in a puddle by his blue
Mercedes. Ten minutes we spend as he attempts wit with a
story of a time he ran out of gas, in a company car, the digital
display telling him he had 52 miles of gas left. He jumped a
highway cement barricade, ripped his stone Dockers, and asked
a farmer for a gas can; then sped back on the road to a meeting
in Pittsburgh, a tall glass building, shattered business deals.
But, my mind

is still with the farmer, whose gas tank
stays full. A life quiet as he picks
brick mortar from his thick fingers
after a quick fix to a corner of the house
clipped by his son the first time he backed
the tractor in. He smiles through crooked
whiskers, whistles with the drum
of the motor in his muddy pick-up.
It's the first day of spring,
first day he can drive with windows down
thinking of big things, like the flap of red
ribbons in his daughter's hair
as she leaps from home to color
another day, another leap above
her father, toward another life
where she can surround herself
with white carpets, red bricks,
and another acquaintance's birthday party
filled with small talk and little room to dream
about the sway of blue grass

in her father's field and the way
it tickled her thighs the first
summer she kissed Paul on
an old burlap blanket, flapping
like a flag on the cracked earth.

—

II

Unnatural

A boy asks if he can marry the family's cat. He figures
it's love: the way the cat bats his palm, the static tingle
when he touches the cat's furry belly, the firm head
rubbing against his taut shin. It's bright green eyes,
wet with lust, and a tail that curls like a question mark
vibrating through the air...

His mother laughs, exclaiming, What did I do wrong?
The stiff whiskers quiver on her lip. She pets her boy's
orange tuft of hair, pulls him to her round, soft belly.
At least he'd be close to home...

The father of the repressed house, whose flaccid penis
ripples like a flag from the poles of his legs, proclaims,
No boy will marry a pussy under my roof. It's not
practical. Think of those sharp front teeth, their
playful snap. All the staccato scrapes he'll have to
cover with band-aids each morning...

The boy sighs, disappointed. His pudgy fingers
wrestle through bright flames of orange fur. The
house cat purrs in his lap, happy under the finesse of
his innocent caress...

—

Le Premier Petit Mort

Suddenly, this boy's life is all in black and white. A fan
rips silent circles across white boards in the ceiling. Its
shadows suddenly black blades across his throat. Sweat
drips like white sap from his ripped chest. A boy
kneels in front of him, silent as a bullet shot through a
white-feathered pillow. The black throat fills with
white lust. This boy's suddenly light as a feather, stiff
as a board, floating into the gray sky...

Capitalist Sex

He secretly envies girls we call sluts.
Hunched in a corner of his bed, he sighs
at models, breasts and pussies waxed in photographs:
one, a Playboy bunny at Christmas, merry
in her white fur bra, panties trimmed in gold.
He dreams of all the money

his body can bring him, all the money
stuffed in G-strings, left on night stands. His slut
aspirations make him proud, a golden
boy, whose practiced tongue finds ecstatic sighs
in every man, leaving them spent and merry
as kids at Christmas, grinning in family photographs.

Naked in his room, he snaps photographs
of his body parts, labels each with the amount of money
it's worth. Legs, $19.99. His mother, Mary,
crinkles her ten cent nose when she catches his slutty
behavior. *Sex is worthless*, she sighs
Look where it got me, a ray of gold

sun dimming behind her; the ugly, golden
years of her life dawning. Old photographs
display her as a shining bride, no signs
of cheap wrinkles, her body now used, no money
down, no interest left in her. *I am a slut,
Ma*, he sneers. *And I've got a little Mary*

in me too, you know what I mean? He merrily
prances out the door, counts his golden
lips and other assets. A homeless slut
now, he cashes in his youth. Clubs pay for photos
of him. In backrooms, men shove money
in his pockets as they shove in him a sigh

of relief. Crouched in public parks, he learns signs
shady men on their lunch breaks use. Mostly married,
they offer him a warm ten minutes, and some money
if they can fuck him bareback, or piss a golden
stream in his mouth. *Can I take your photograph?*
one of them asks. *For a website, 'Fresh Young Sluts.'*

Yes, he sighs. Now, men pay $9.95, with Visa Gold
cards, for a merry moment lit by his photograph:
a boy with nothing, no money, but his hard earned title *slut*.

—

How Soon is Now?

It is the last time I see him. Head just shaved
t-shirt littered with tiny clips of brown hair
like intentional dandruff on his shoulders.
He finally smiles after two Sam Adams
breath seeps across the table
with a saltiness of pumpkin seeds and stale beer.
His attention is a slowly receding tide.
It coats me in a thin, cool spray I try to grip
like a blanket bunched at my chin.
You knew I was never *that way*, he says.
His thin eyes, a piercing azure, ripple as a shell might
skipping on the Caribbean Sea.
On a jukebox, Morrissey's voice trembles
over a quivering bass line, just as it did
when we laid in our old bed, damp sheets pressed
against my chest, their wrinkly cotton leaving lines
crushed into my untouched skin.
We get up, exit the musty bar. The hot vinyl seat
sears it folds into the backs of my legs.
As I rub the creased redness, he waves goodbye,
the friction warming my thighs
as the bite of autumn swells around me.

—

Older Man, One Night Stand

Drifting through Cuban
jazz in your dining
room, paintings in your
living room, scraped knees
on the Berber by
your couch, romancing
framed newspaper columns
in your bathroom - I
only remember
the doorknob in your
bedroom - though you tried
so hard to converse
as we walked to the
Metro, I already
was driving home in
my mind still missing
the piece I thought you'd
fit in me.

Safer Sex

We meet in the morning, in the still
under construction house you're working on.

Stepping through sawdust
the stone etched chest of David

greets us. Plaster dust
flirts with our nostrils, tickles

throats. On sanded stairs
before a bedroom is discovered

I cross the tangled welcome mat
above your penis, hard

like a steel crane hoisting me
onto blue sheet waves in your waterbed

naked but for gray argyle socks
that escape our undressing game.

Careful, I say, as you bend me
and I take your cock and all your fucks

into me. I think, only this green
sheath of rubber between us

can't protect from all this dust
you stir, all these nails you pound in me.

Attempts at Goodbye

There are two boys who don't know the word
goodbye. After sex finishes, their pants and sweat
hushed between soft sheets, one attempts sleep on the
naked mattress. The other, restless, paces around the
bed, attempts to pack a soft suitcase. He folds a white
sweater and attempts surrender, setting it on the bed
like a white flag...

The sweater ignored, he attempts sitting in ribbons of
moonlight spread wildly over a soft leather chair. The
boys don't move for hours, afraid to say what rests in
eddies of dust, under the soft quilted night. They
think even blinking will wave the light illuminating
them...

They pull soft clothes on, like tight nylon over sun-
burned flesh. The bright moon glaring, tangled in
black branches with buds bitten by late April frost. It
casts bars over their big lips. It's easy to lock words
under tongues like pearls...

—

Feed Like Babies

My nephew suckles
on a rubber nipple.
The warm milk just gone
as his mouth wilts and dribbles
opaque beads on his dimpled chin.
His eyes drift up and he sleeps
in my arms. Later,
I want his peace,
so I spill my clothes
on another stranger's floor,
curl between his legs
until my tired jaw sags.
Lips won't purse tight enough
around his hard cock.
It grows as he closes his eyes,
clamped shut, turned up, away from me.
His moans tell me, *soon, stay with me*
in this rhythm. Instead,
I give him my hand
gripped and lubed with spit,
rest my head on his hard
thigh, close my eyes
and dream of a restaurant
designed so that I am cradled
on my back, a long
pillow under me
stuffed with muscular cushions.
Food, liquid and milky,
slides into my mouth
through supple nipples
suspended above my head.
I open my eyes,
look up at him dozing now,
his semen spilt.
It drips on his splayed thigh
and I slip away into a blushed
morning. The sun's glow,
a warning of late afternoon rain.

I slop through it,
wet and alone, empty
and hungry for more.

—

Before Dinner

On a solid table, start with ironed
linens, easy to clean of stains.

Rub spoons with fog of breath,
glint them across your thigh.

Then knives, watch blades like fast silver
tongues kiss edges of plates.

Two forks, one for this first
course, one for the next.

Stroke napkins and fold them
to wait for a warm lap to cradle.

The crystal wine glasses, touch
their rims softly, move a finger

around and around
listen to them sing.

Push your chair in,
Pull your guest's out.

Take a candle stick, its wick cut, held erect
between the tip of two licked fingers

and light the flame.

Fairy Tale

The sun sets slowly now. No more stars
to wish upon, only flesh and each glint

of sweat on your brow. Your sweatshirt hugs me.
Its wool prickly like the hairs on your chest.

Blood shines under taut skin, like that first night
I signed your inner thigh with my tongue,

kissed the weak spot on the underbelly
of your past. I found love jammed in the back

of your throat, dancing between your toes,
tried to dig it out just beneath all your

surfaces. Then, the we just slipped in me,
like sleep, deep and comforting. You wake.

Our pages turning quickly. It's not
that we have melded, or carried

one another off, but just that our bodies
fit together so tightly and some moments

there are less than two of us in the room.

—

Sonnet #1: For Sanford

after Pablo Neruda's first "Cien sonetos de amor"

Sanford: the name of beach, or a shell, or a plane,
of things that pierce the sky, and expand:
word in whose firmament my road leads,
in whose dusty trails I hitchhike home.

Wild reeds sway in the breeze of that name,
with sun-tanned hills of Toulouse behind them:
its letters are the marrow of your sternum
that lets my head rest firmly in the center of you.

O name that unwraps a hundred gifts in each syllable
like crisp morning coffee
in the brash light of the city.

Wrestle me with your muscular love; load me
with your bullet eyes, if you want - only let me
dance like a reed in the wind of your name, let me breathe there.

—

Restricted Union

after Andre Breton's "Free Union"

My lover whose toes are snowflakes scattering in gated fields of flesh
Whose ankles bend like crowded streets jammed with cars and curbs
Whose wrists fall limp like an Osprey's wing curving through gray clouds
Whose voice is deep shades of forests, echoing at dusk to answer the Veery's
    secretive song
Whose voice is blue and long, a Coltrane's *Love Supreme*, hushed and jumping
    from strict bars of musical staffs
Whose hair is black asphalt covered in snow
Whose heart rustles its neck feathers, fans its tail, arches down wings
    like a caged ricebird, alone in its mating dance
Whose lips are Wisteria withering in shade from a field of September Bluestems
My lover whose ass is two children blowing gum bubbles, the pink globes
    pressing together until they burst
Whose hands hold love like swamp vines hang lavender flowers over enveloping
    waters
Whose eyes hold rivers of blood like rubies blistering in caves
Whose thoughts are stars that glow from millions of years ago
Whose mouth is a wet clock that ticks kisses like seconds
Whose tongue is a silk scarf tightened around a slender neck
Whose eyelashes are winter branches blanched with snow
My lover whose eyebrows are ancient arcs of triumph
Whose temples are pressed wood, kneaded and sanded to a sheen
Whose shoulders are hilly slopes with tiny skiers pinned among pines
Whose fingers are the spokes of flame in a field of burning crosses
Whose fingers are ballet legs contracted in controlled leaps
Whose armpits are ashen pits of a moon crater
Whose arms are water left after tides wash back to sea, licking the sand clean
Whose legs are wild sunflowers in August, crowded under a French sky
My lover whose feet are books coded in Braille
Whose neck is a stolen lick of cherry popsicle in summer
Whose throat is an ancient alphabet locked in a mountainous tomb
Whose chest is a scrubbed board on a cruise ship deck, speckled with sand
    from tourists' tanned feet
Whose back is a city skyline receding from the boxed view of an airplane window
My lover with thighs that light dark places like spotlights circling a prison field
Whose asshole is a pink Cosmopolitan, still stirring in its cone glass
Whose cock is the pen that frees these words, the musical note held beyond breath
My lover whose breath is a blanket against the beating world

In a Picture, Two Gay Men Before AIDS

inhale laughter, faces red with the freedom
of desire. Supple fingers flex across a chest,
flip open each button under a tan
cashmere sweater, run freely on a bare
field of flesh, down, down, to a trail of dark
brown hair, grip a choice weapon. Lips
stretched in grins touch, puff and pop kisses
around smooth chins, strong dimples.

They lean into one another, the easy space between them
closes. After the flash of the camera's bulb
darkens, they will hug, move to a bedroom,
where they catch each other's breaths, unbuckle
shoes, lips suckle sturdy nipples. In their mouths
both heap and shake, spit a white love that splashes
in corners of lips and falls effortlessly down throats.
The men swoon, spoon until morning in a bed

where two years later, they will wake, soaked in night sweats,
a mouth coated in white thrush, a quick rush
to the bathroom, and a lover, left alone, lit only by the glow
that still emits from a photo of their first laugh, framed
and resting like a tombstone on their shared nightstand.

—

Laramie

Smudged in the middle
of America. Matthew, parts
of you still hang there

on wood. Bound ankles.
Blood stained plaid. Head gashed.
Wind still taunts and yells.

We'll teach ya, faggot,
disgusting pig. Make him squeal.
Clouds   spit   spit   spit

spread the hate. Matthew,
we become pieces of you everyday.
On streets in Detroit,

Tom and I drive, hold hands,
windows down. Brown van
pulls up, rust seeps on its sides.

We hear deep laughs,
sharp glances. Automatically,
no words, our hands part, rest safely

on our own laps,
until the light turns. Their rust
speeds away, leaves a trail

of fumes. Our hands grasp
squeeze a little tighter.
Exhale, this time.

III

Shaving My Father

It is a new intimacy between us,
more like a soldier who lies naked on
another soldier to bring him back from
icy waters, than any of the ways
I know to be intimate with a man.

I lean in, inches from his face, this close
for the first time in too many years.
His breath smells of stale ginger, biting
sweetness of aluminum. He tells me
twice how mother likes the card I bought for her.

He never taught me to shave, never stood
with me in a mirror, telling me where
to stretch my skin or switch the razor
direction, which way to tilt my head.
He flinches each time I touch his face.

Not until now do I begin to learn
his skin, barely opaque, thin as tissue
paper. Skin that knew the feel of the first
disposable razors and bought toilet
paper to cover small cuts, small mistakes.

This close, I even memorize his breath,
mimic his staccato inhales and
extended exhales, his silent admission
of how quickly life came into him,
and how slowly he is letting it out.

Monogram

The sweater is ready to be found
after a long wait in the musty chest of drawers,
like a Christmas gift my dad cannot give me.

It smells of mostly old pressed wood,
but closer I can waft the scent
off its cigarette burns and whiskey stains,

feel the faint breeze of a golf course
and the linger of Brut cologne,
the first smell of men I knew.

I am in love with its color, an orange
that no longer exists, the fading tan
of my Cherokee grandma in late October.

Putting it on is uncomfortable
stiff like my dad's hugs
more gruff wool and acrylic, no cotton.

My hand smoothes its wrinkles, stops
to outline his initials, resting on my chest,
stitched in tan thread so permanently.

I decide to never take it off
as if somehow it can sew us together,
burn his monogram deep within me.

Night Watch

I.

Night is a criminal. It steals
the flap of plastic daisies
in bike spokes, a dog's bark.
Light rain falls, chiffon curtains
line windows. Table lamps
look like candle flickers.

A man sits in his tan Buick,
gas taps at garage walls.
He breathes deeply, unlocks his lungs
for Night to come filch them of air.

II.

I enter the hospital room.
My right hand grips
a ripe orange. My mother,
face full of new wrinkles,
fills a chair in the corner.
"I will be here, all night," I say.

She lifts a corner of her mouth
packs books and used tissues
in a canvas bag, pushes
her arms through coat sleeves,
folds a scarf across her chest
making a silent sign of the cross.

She touches the cold nose
of my father, balances
just above his lips.
A second later, she leaves,
Night close behind,
pilfering through her memories.

III.

The Buick runs out of gas. It takes longer
than he expects to asphyxiate himself.
Night slices his breath, purloins
his angry screams into empty pockets.

IV.

There are hours, no changes.
Medicine drips into my father,
his eyes dip closed, then open,
breath thumps. At 2am, I peel the orange.
It stings the air with citrus,
pokes tiny needles in my torn cuticles.

My father's eyes open, catch mine.
Night slips in, robs his skin of color
'til it's chalky as the underside
of the orange rind clinging to my hand.

V.

After Night finishes, the man sits
dead in his Buick and brown cardigan.
His kids find him, his face full of air
a purple party balloon, stretched and sheen,

that bobs through their heads at night
as the blackness spreads over us
stealing the warm, comfortable light of day.

—

B

The last word my father never said
began with the letter "B." His breath
was too drained to press it out. I cradled
his worn bald head in my warm palm.

It was supple, like a baby's, staring
at me with the deep, innocent blue
pools of his eyes, trying to push out
a single word. I, like a doting

parent, was waiting on proud breath and
anticipatory tears for that sound
to complete itself, to form a word,
a memento. B. Was he calling

me his boy, one last time? Saying a simple
"bye"? Teaching me to drive in a tan
Buick. Were the bombs of the Pacific
echoing in his head? Did he long

for the bread of church or his sacred
booze? Maybe he was already resting
on a beach in the Bahamas with
his second bride, or finishing the back

nine with Bobbie. What did he believe in?
Was he realizing he was in
the halls of Beaumont where he met his
Mary and was losing his life?

At the end, my sister and I
rested our hands on him, after
words had already left
and he was chasing them quickly away.

I was filled with his B's.
One letter and the endless
questions never answered.

Father's Day Dream

My first book of poems is published
on Carr's gourmet crackers. At its debut,
women in pleather mini-dresses
pose with men in shining button-downs.
They sample stanzas with Brie and artichoke hearts.
My words dissolve on their tongues, stick
between their teeth. Is poetry as pointless
as party appetizers? I wander

into my mother's kitchen, the crowd's
din echoes behind me. Alone, I crumble
down to a salty mess of tears. Father
stumbles in, still in loose cotton pajamas, a crusty
flannel robe that gapes open like a dead man's
mouth. His skin already coated in ashy
cells, dry from the chemo drip attached
to his right arm. He lugs the IV pole
behind him. Shaky, dad grips my shoulders
in a hug and says, *Eating your poems is a gift.*

I wake, drenched in my own
regret. My father, still ashes stuffed
in a cardboard box, buried only under
condolence cards, old photos. Three days
before my second Father's Day without him,
and me, still worried about the gifts
I didn't give him.

The Drunk

The party spills out
onto a dirty street in Detroit,
an apocalyptic parking lot,
a line of shaking lights and broken bulbs
seethe against the blacked out night.
Specks of garbage float in liquid summer air
like dislodged stars wandering the city
in search for last call.
On the curb by our black Jetta
a bum, delirious for a drink,
croons a broken tune too loudly,
like a man with headphones
who doesn't realize no one else hears the music.
He sings of opening the clouds
and falling into a cotton candy sleep.
His scent hits our nostrils
like the gamy crawl of a B & G Merlot
before the bruised liquid crosses your lips.
I'm drunk too, the spice of rum pungent
on my sugary tongue, and through the squint
of my eyes, swollen with bar smoke
I wonder if it's my dad
slumped over the broken slab of concrete
brought back from his poisoned death
to live life like he wanted
drunk and alone
waiting for the next drink.
At home, I cuddle next to my lover,
my mouth rinsed and scoured
with antiseptic, my skin cleaned
of the tobacco haze that seeps
from our clothes, slumped in a pile
on our hardwood floors.
The room spins and I curl away
into myself, hoping the stench
of my drunk blood stays buried
in a grave I never visit.

acknowledgements

Grateful acknowledgement is made to the editors of the following journals and publications in which some of these poems or earlier versions of them first appeared:

Blaze: "At the Airport," "La Fin du Monde,"
   "Suppose At Twelve, I Am Not a Boy"
Connecticut River Review: "B"
Metro Times: "Older Man, One Night Stand,"
   "13th Street Nursery Rhyme"
Paterson Literary Review: "Shaving My Father"
Rattle: "Out of My Mother"

"Shaving My Father" also received a Commendation Award in the 2001 Allen Ginsberg Poetry Awards. "Restricted Union" received Third Place in the 2003 Writer's Voice of Metropolitan Detroit's Poetry Contest, judged by X.J. Kennedy.

To my partner, Sanford, for giving me the two greatest gifts: his love and the freedom to chase the crazy words that run through my head all day long.

To the members of the Emerging Ink Collective (formerly Walloon Alumni Writer's Group), Cheri, Katie, Lisa, Lori and Randy, for having just as many crazy words to chase, but also for having the compassionate leashes that help reel them in and turn them into art.

To my Mom, Mary, and sister, Jennifer, for nurturing my old soul with unconditional love, a lot of hugs, and the belief that we can survive anything.

To all my dear friends, too numerous to name, for never blinking whenever I said I wanted to be a poet.

To ML Liebler, without whom, at the least, it would have taken me many more years to find poetry and its magic. Your undying support is always with me, and I hope I can return it someday.

To Kat, for your generous time, good conversation, and talent.

In loving memory of my father, Pierce.

about the author

Steven Rydman was born, raised and still resides in the Metropolitan Detroit area of Michigan. He holds a B.S. Degree (Suma Cum Laude) from Wayne State University in Secondary Education English and Math. For three years, he worked for the Midwest AIDS Prevention Project, traveling the state of Michigan and beyond doing fundraising, safer sex workshops and gay/lesbian sensitivity trainings. He left that job in 2001 to concentrate on his writing full-time. In December 2002, he began a Masters of Fine Arts in Poetry at Antioch University Los Angeles in their low-residency program, which will be completed in December 2004.